Look To This Day

A KEEPSAKE OF JOYFUL AND INSPIRING THOUGHTS

♛

Hallmark Editions

If you would have a mind at peace,
  A heart that cannot harden,
  Go find a door that opens wide
  Upon a lovely garden.

Inscription at Cypress Gardens

LITTLE THINGS

Sometimes we may not realize
    that everything we do
  Affects not only our lives
    but touches others, too.
  A single happy smile
    can always brighten up the day
  For anyone who happens
    to be passing by your way,
  And a little bit of thoughtfulness
    that shows someone you care
  Creates a ray of sunshine
    for both of you to share.

Karen Ravn

THE SALUTATION OF THE DAWN

Listen to the exhortation of the dawn!
Look to this day! For it is life,
The very life of life.
In its brief course lie all the varieties
And realities of your existence.
The bliss of growth,
The glory of action,
The splendor of beauty,
For yesterday is but a dream,
And tomorrow is only a vision:
But today well lived
Makes every yesterday a dream of happiness,
And every tomorrow a vision of hope.
Look well, therefore, to this day!
Such is the salutation of the dawn.

from the Sanskrit

"Take your needle...and work at your pattern;
it will come out a rose by and by."
Life is like that;
one stitch at a time taken patiently,
and the pattern will come out all right
like the embroidery.

Oliver Wendell Holmes

LIFE IS GOOD

Let me not fail to find that life is good.
Though storms may rage around me, and the dark
Press close upon the heights whereon I've stood,
Let me lift up a song as does the lark
Sure of the warming sunlight when the shower
Is done, and rainbow beauty rims the hill,
For nothing hinders God's almighty power
To summon blessings where and how He will.

From out the stormiest place, the darkest deep,
At His great word a steadfast friend may come,
Or from the loss that once I stayed to weep,
A shining blessing greater than the sum
Of all my woes. I need but take His hand
To see life fair, to see it whole and new,
Touched with His matchless glory, like a land
Of promise such as eager pilgrims view.
I need but trust His love, as all men should,
To know with joy and faith that life is good.

Eleanor Halbrook Zimmerman

Let us be of good cheer,
   remembering that the misfortunes hardest to bear
         are those which never come.

James Russell Lowell

He who has not spent hours, days, or years
with someone he loves cannot know what happiness is,
for he is unable to imagine a protracted miracle like this --
one which makes out of ordinary sights and
events the most enchanted existence.

André Maurois

The sunshine of life
is made up of very little beams
that are bright all the time.

Aiken

Now the sun is rising
calm and bright;
The birds are singing…
The sky rejoices….
All things
that love the sun
are out-of-doors.

William Wordsworth

Nature is painting for us, day after day, pictures
of infinite beauty if only we have the eyes to see them.

John Ruskin

When I listen to the music of life,
I'm able to join in the dancing.

Katherine Long

Let us believe
what we do not see and know.
Let us forestall knowledge by faith.
Let us maintain
before we have demonstrated.
This seeming paradox
is the secret of happiness....
We do all things in this world by faith
in the word of others....
Why should we be unwilling
to use for heavenly objects
what we daily use for earthly?

John Henry Newman

Happiness is a butterfly
which when pursued is just beyond your grasp…
but if you will sit down quietly,
may alight upon you.

Nathaniel Hawthorne

To accomplish great things,
we must not only act but also dream,
not only plan but also believe.

Anatole France

ESSENTIALS

Plus-production, rocket-speeds,
strive and struggle, push and climb,
when all a human creature needs
is love and laughter--and more time.

Dorothy Brown Thompson

Reverence is one of the signs of strength;
　　　　irreverence one of the surest indications of weakness.
No man will rise high who jeers at sacred things.
　　　　The fine loyalties of life must be reverenced
　　　　　　or they will be foresworn in the day of trial.

Author Unknown

I have always believed that good
　　　　　　is only beauty put into practice.

Jean Jacques Rousseau

The more faithfully you listen to the voice within you,
　　the better you will hear what is sounding outside.

Dag Hammarskjold

Let there be many windows in your soul,
　　　　That all the glory of the universe
　　　　May beautify it.

Ella Wheeler Wilcox

THE MAKING OF FRIENDS

Life is sweet just because of the friends we have made
And the things which in common we share;
We want to live on, not just for ourselves,
But because of the people who care;
It's giving and doing for somebody else...
On that all life's splendor depends,
And the joy of this world when you've summed it all up,
Is found in the making of friends.

Edgar A. Guest

I still find each day too short
        for all the thoughts I want to think,
        all the walks I want to take,
        all the books I want to read,
        and all the friends I want to see.
    The longer I live the more my mind dwells
        upon the beauty and the wonder of the world.

John Burroughs

It is the nature of love to work in a thousand different ways.

Saint Teresa

PRAYER

Give us a leaf and a star,
A bar of light through the trees:
Visible entities
To prove that You are.

Give us a leaf and a star,
And the sun and the thunder,
Awaken our wonder,
Our sleeping awareness.

Give us a flower
To tell of Your power.

Give us a leaf and a star,
And all of earth's spectacular
Creations...
Nature's wonder
To astound us;
The mantle of Your peace
Around us.

Katherine Nelson Davis

NO RESERVATION

I swept my heart of bitterness,
Then hung a sign, "For Rent,"
And every room was occupied
Before the day was spent.

The first I gave to Gallantry--
I always shall be glad;
To Worship and to Prayer I gave
The finest rooms I had.

Service took one apartment, but
I saved the space above
For Faith and Purity and Hope,
For Wisdom, Truth, and Love.

An old acquaintance came at dusk--
I turned the sign about.
"My heart is very full," I said.
"I've no room for you, Doubt."

Nina Stiles

A year is…
the sparkle of snowflakes,
the sweet melody of robins,
the fragrance of roses,
and the gold and ruby
of fallen leaves.

A year is three hundred sixty-five days of beauty…
Three hundred sixty-five reasons for joy.

Tina Hacker

BIRD IN THE AUTUMN

He finds a scanty shelter
In trees grown gay, but thinned.
He feels the breath of winter
That edges every wind.

But well he knows that somewhere
Eternal summer sings,
The sky is wide for journeys,
And all God's birds have wings.

Clara Aiken Speer

ALONE WITH NATURE

The best remedy for those who are afraid, lonely, or unhappy is to go outside, somewhere where they can be quite alone with the heavens, nature, and God. Because only then does one feel that all is as it should be and that God wishes to see people happy, amidst the simple beauty of nature. As long as this exists, and it certainly always will, I know that then there will always be comfort for every sorrow, whatever the circumstances may be.

Anne Frank

Though we travel the world over to find the beautiful,
we must carry it with us or we will find it not.

Ralph Waldo Emerson

WHAT IS HAPPINESS?

The life that matters is all around you, in the flowers of your garden, in the little lizard sunning himself on your balcony, in the children looking tenderly at their mother, in the embracing lovers, in the house where a family eats and loves and plays games together. Nothing is more important than these humble lives which, added together, make up humanity.

André Maurois

Very little is needed to make a happy life.
It is all within yourself, in your way of thinking.

Marcus Aurelius

CYCLE

"It will be good," he said, "this land
    When I have cleared the stone."
Then stooping back and calloused hand
    Piled up his walls, alone.

His great-granddaughter came last fall
    And found the prospect drear....
"I know," she cried. "We'll spread this wall
    And make rock-gardens here!"

Dorothy Brown Thompson

Happy times and bygone days are never lost....
In truth, they grow more wonderful
within the heart that keeps them.

Kay Andrew

DANDELIONS

What child hasn't picked them once
or taken home bouquets,
whistled through their hollow stems
on lazy, sunny days,
braided sticky necklaces
or made a friendship ring?

What child hasn't blown the puff
to watch the seeds take wing
...from these golden buttons
sewn upon the coat of Spring?

Mary A. Loberg

Learn the sweet magic of a cheerful face —
       Not always smiling, but at least serene.

Oliver Wendell Holmes

Walk on a rainbow trail;
    walk on a trail of song,
    and all about you will be beauty.
There is a way out of every dark mist,
    over a rainbow trail.

Navajo Song

Life is the love that reaches out
      building bridges
    across gulfs of uncertainty…
to touch hands, hearts and souls
    in the experience of union.

Peter Seymour

TOY BALLOONS

Great globes of color lift and glitter —
   But glory's ownership is bitter.

   Our childhood learned, from that first clutch,
   Joy dies from loving it too much.

   Now, wise to savor what life brings,
   We are content to hold taut strings

   But never grasp the rainbow sweep.
   Bright wonder was not meant to keep.
                          Dorothy Brown Thompson

I am not afraid of tomorrow,
         for I have seen yesterday and I love today.
                          William Allen White

Kindness in words creates confidence,
         Kindness in thinking creates profoundness,
         Kindness in giving creates love.
                          Lao-Tse

Each day is a lifetime in miniature…To awaken each morning is to be born again, to fall asleep at night is to die to the day. In between waking and sleeping are the golden hours of the day. What we cannot do for a lifetime we can do for a daytime. "Anyone," wrote Robert Louis Stevenson, "can live sweetly, patiently, lovingly, purely, till the sun goes down." Anyone can hold his temper for a day and guard the words he speaks. Anyone can carry his burden heroically for one day. Anyone can strive to be happy for a day and to spread happiness around. Anyone can radiate love for a day.

Anyone can rise above fear for a day and meet each situation with courage. Anyone can be kind and thoughtful and considerate for a day. Anyone can endeavor to learn something new each day and mark some growth. When we fail and fall short, let us forgive ourselves and consider the words of Emerson: "Finish every day and be done with it. Tomorrow is a new day; you will begin it well and serenely and with too high a spirit to be cumbered by your old nonsense." Live a day at a time and remember that tomorrow is another today.

Wilferd A. Peterson

Every noble work is at first 'impossible'. In very truth, for every noble work the possibilities will lie diffused through immensity; inarticulate, undiscoverable, except to faith. Like Gideon, thou shalt spread out thy fleece at the door of thy tent; see whether under the wide arch of heaven there be any bounteous moisture, or none.

Carlyle

Having done all thou canst do, await the event with a calm mind. Whatever it be, thou art blameless, and safe therefore from harm.

If we except the present instant, which is gone before we can call attention to it, all time is past, since the future does not exist. What is past has ceased to be; and the whole of life, therefore, is summed up in an instant, which — if we try to think of it — vanishes. It is this which insight into the illusiveness, the evanescence, the emptiness, the futility of temporal existence, driving the soul back on itself and impelling it to seek escape from annihilation in the bosom of the Eternal, in which, and not in time, it truly lives.

John Lancaster Spalding

A child said, What is the grass?
       fetching it to me with full hands…
I guess it is the handkerchief of the Lord.

Walt Whitman

A HAPPY THOUGHT

I searched the world
For a happy thought
   And gave up
   In despair--
Until I climbed a grassy hill
And found a bluebird there!

Boyd R. Ogden

I live in a very small house,
       but my windows look out
    on a very large world.

Confucius

For me it is enough to say
That something beautiful passed my way.

Ida Catherine Rohlf

from A CREED

There is a destiny that makes us brothers;
None goes his way alone:
All that we send into the lives of others
Comes back into our own.

Edwin Markham

Little deeds of kindness,
Little words of love,
Help to make earth happy
Like the Heaven above!

Julia Fletcher Carney

SEA GULL

Bird born above the need for singing,
 Born for soaring, dipping, swinging,
 Wheeling out an arc of sky
 With your strange, triumphal cry...
 Now brushing cloud, now skimming sea,
 Brave gull, aloof and proudly free!
 As you span the current's buoyant air,
 My soul soars to meet you there!
Mary R. Hurley

Bright thoughts, clear deeds, constancy,
 fidelity, bounty and generous honesty
are the gems of noble minds.
Sir Thomas Browne

My business is not to remake myself,
but to make the absolute best of what God made.
Robert Browning

I discovered the secret of the sea
in meditation upon the dewdrop.
Kahlil Gibran

31

STEPPING-STONES

I struggled to move boulders
And many an obstacle
Out of my way.
I wore myself out
Pressing against them,
Pushing in vain;
Then wept at my own inadequacy
And their relentless strength.

And then, one spring morning,
I listened to the birds and felt refreshed
Watching their trusting flight
Above the dangers and the discontents.
"Oh, to have wings," I prayed.
"But you have feet," the answer came.
"Were they not meant to climb?
And hands, are they not able to cling?
I have put stepping-stones for you
And rocky promontories fitted to your hand.
Look up and scale the heights."
And lo! my obstacles,
Which I had tried to shove out of my way,
Were stones to climb upon
Out of the marshy bog.

And from each one another came to view,
And none of them was singly hard to reach.
And when they seemed too steep,
I stretched my hand above
To feel it close upon a firm, strong aid,
And laughed to think I was so blind
A few short suns before.

Gertrude Helen Crawford

Joy sings in beauty that surrounds us…
Joy smiles through loved ones all around us…
Joy speaks in gentle words that guide us…
Joy smiles in feelings deep inside us.

Barbara Burrow

HAPPY IS THE HEART

Happy is the heart that sings!
Thanking God for little things,
Finding courage where a hill
Lifts its everlasting will,
Saying, when the night is dark,
"Morning cometh, and the lark!"

Happy is the heart that knows
Close communion with the rose,
Taking pleasure in the way
God has clothed a summer day,
Saying, when the clouds complain,
"There's a rainbow in the rain!"

Vivian Yeiser Laramore

The happiest people seem to be those
    who have no particular cause for being happy
    except the fact that they are so....

Dean William Ralph Inge

THE CHILD'S QUESTION

Will there really be a "Morning"?
    Is there such a thing as "Day"?
    Could I see it from the mountains
    If I were as tall as they?

Has it feet like Water lilies?
    Has it feathers like a Bird?
    Is it brought from famous countries
    Of which I have never heard?

Oh, some Scholar! Oh, some Sailor,
    Oh, some Wise Man from the skies!
    Please to tell a little Pilgrim
    Where the place called "Morning" lies?

Emily Dickinson

YOUNG TREES

A young tree standing
  Slim and still
  Is a tall green flower
  On a quiet hill.

A young tree bending
Along a lane
Is a green flame blowing
In wind and rain.

A young tree growing
In any weather
By a silver barn
Is an emerald feather.

My heart grows breathless
When I pass by
A young tree reaching
Toward a golden sky,

Or stretching upward,
Brave and proud,
To toss its branches
Against a cloud.

Frances Frost

Can you sing as well as did Caruso? Can you paint as exquisitely as did Raphael? Can you release beautiful forms from their marble prisons as well as did Michelangelo? Can you sway the masses with your silver-tongued oratory as did Disraeli, or Beecher? Can you make your pen mightier than the sword?

Anyone can ask a flock of questions, like the above, and the answer may be simple. It is likely "No." But in fairness to yourself review these thoughts: A daisy cannot bring the price for an American Beauty rose. A meadowlark cannot outsing a nightingale. The moon cannot shine as brightly as the sun. An automobile cannot cover as much distance in a day as an airplane.

But we should not forget that the humble daisy by the wayside has cheered many load-weary travelers. Common birds bring joy and gladness to many hearts as they fill the air with sweet song. The moon has served to bring joy to myriads of lonely souls. And the automobile is still a very useful tool.

The place in life you aspire to fill has no greater exactions than you are able to meet, if you strive hard enough. Remember, "the mighty oak started out as a nut." Lift where you stand. Be the best of which you are capable. Try each day to make a smile grow where nary a one grew before. And with each low descending sun there will be at least two people in the world who will be glad and one of them will be you.

John Edwin Price

They tell of Adam:

How frightened he must have been when, for the first time, he saw the sun disappear, ending the light of day.

It was Adam's first *darkness!*

How could he understand the night, when he had never seen a dawn?

After the splendor of the sun, how astonishingly dark the darkness was; how desperate the long terror of the first fall of night...until Adam learned that *day* would come again: that there is order in the universe.

And then Adam could begin to see how much light *remains* in the sky at night: the stars, and their enduring promise of the sun...

The returning star of day.

Adam learned *the night is never wholly dark, and no night is endless*...even as each of us must learn it in our own times of trouble and of darkness.

The light is never far.

The Jewish Theological Seminary of America

Today is the first day of the rest of your life.
Charles A. Dederich

ME

As long as I live
I shall always be
My Self--and no other,
Just me.

Like a tree--
Willow, elder,
Aspen, thorn,
Or cypress forlorn.

Like a flower,
For its hour
Primrose, or pink,
Or a violet--
Sunned by the sun,
And with dewdrops wet.

Always just me.
Walter de la Mare

D awn!
  Is there a time so pure so ripe with possibilities?
  This is the hour--Seize the day!
  Robert Wood

LILIES OF THE VALLEY

When lilies of the valley bloom,
Their purity and grace
Uplift my heart and make the world
A joyful, lovely place.

I kneel down softly where they grow
And listen till I almost hear
The fairy music of their bells
Chiming soft and clear.

Jane Merchant

W hatsoever things are lovely...
            think on these things.
  Philippians 4:8

THE WATER LILIES

Along a dim, secluded trail, one day,
Deep in the shadows of a quiet wood,
I saw a pool where water lilies lay,
Flowering, it seemed, in lonely solitude.

But ah, not so! Their petals lured the breeze
To pause and kiss them on its restless flight,
They flaunted beauty for the encircling trees
And kept a tryst with stars each silver night.

Each blossom like a chalice held the dew,
For them the water sang its lullaby,
They heard the matins of the birds and knew
The benediction of the evening sky.

Kay Wissinger

PRAYER WITHOUT WORDS

A thought slides over where words fear,
Lest sound dissolve the gathering tear,
  Two hands praying, find and reach
  Stars beyond the sky of speech.

Gladys McKee

LINES FROM A WINDOW

The morning,
   quiet,
   brought the day to me
   I received it with love
   and never gave it back again
   one ought
   to keep a gift.
   The noontime
      baked the sidewalks
      and the leaves.
      I loved the noon
      because it was so alone
      with just
      one thing to do.
      But ah
      the evening
      blue and purple,
      lovely and with hidden
      freshness, brought from the day
      new things.
      The baked leaves stirred
      frogs sang
      the crickets stirred the air
      and the whole choir of birds
      slept.
      How wonderful a world
      where melody can sleep.

Sister Mary Faith, O.S.B.

We planted flowers today, Lord.
My youngest kept calling them "miracles" instead of marigolds.
We laughed and had a wonderful time
together planting your "miracles."
Barbara Burrow

For the heart that is free,
life is a celebration of beauty,
a festival of the spirit.
Edward Cunningham

RECIPE FOR A HAPPY LIFE

Here's a sure-fire recipe for making your own sunshine:
Take equal parts of kindness, unselfishness, thoughtfulness.
Mix with love, and scatter with helpful words.
Add a smile or two.
Throw in a spice of cheerfulness.
Stir with a hearty laugh.
Share with everyone.
Sunshine Magazine

Happiness and Beauty are Love's children.
Rita Hayden

The world is a looking glass, and gives back
to every man the reflection of his own face.
Frown at it, and it in turn will look sourly upon you;
laugh at it and with it, and it is a jolly, kind companion.

William Makepeace Thackeray

Reason is our soul's left hand,
Faith her right.
By these we reach divinity.

John Donne

What is lovely never dies,
But passes into other loveliness,
Stardust, or sea-foam,
flower or winged air.

Aldrich

A sorrow shared is but half a trouble,
but a joy that's shared is a joy made double.
Old Proverb

Hope is itself a species of happiness
and, perhaps,
the chief happiness
which this world affords.
Samuel Johnson

There are two ways
of spreading light:
to be the candle
or the mirror that reflects it.
Edith Wharton

A "THANK-YOU"
CAN BE MANY THINGS

Welcome as the daisies,
Refreshing as summer rains,
Cheery as yellow daffodils
And sunlit windowpanes.
Cherished as a tender kiss,
Friendly as a smile
A "Thank-you"
Can be many things,
Making life
Worthwhile.

Violet Bigelow Rourke

Happiness makes up in height for what it lacks in length.

Robert Frost

The road of life winds on, and we like travelers go
From turn to turn until we come to know
The truth that life is endless....

Martha Smock

Heaven is under our feet as well as over our heads.

Henry David Thoreau

THAT'S HOW THE SUN SHINES

A boy and his father were watching
One day as the sun slowly set.
The rays of the sun on a window
Made a sight they would never forget.

For the glass in the house of a neighbor,
Then appeared as a huge golden plate.
They walked forward to look at it closer;
But they got there a little too late.

For the rays of the sun had moved onward;
So the trip they had made was in vain.
When they turned to go back to their own house;
There was gold on their own windowpane.

Now the sun is forever in motion;
Everyday into lives it will shine.
Today, it may shine in your neighbors'
Tomorrow, in your life or mine.

Don Church

MEDITATIONS OF A HOUSEWIFE

Five yellow rosebuds, in a blue vase,
Perfectly molded, gentle in grace.
Fresh-laundered curtains here by my sink.
There 'neath my window birds pause to drink!
Seven red apples in a glass bowl;
Why do they bless and strengthen my soul?

Clean clothes are hanging here in the sun,
Smelling of pure suds — washing is done!
Draining the tubs, scrubbing the floor,
Dusting the table, answering the door,
Digging the garden, hoeing the weeds;
Why do these duties care for my needs?

Lord, mold me gently, just like the rose,
Cleanse me and keep me clean like my clothes;
Empty my soul of every gross thing,
Clear now my life of habits that cling:
Weed out all error. Lord, let me be
A good-hearted housewife worshiping Thee!

Lydia Stoner

Live with your whole being...
all the days of your life!
Your reward will be true happiness!

Rebecca Thomas Shaw

Success is to be measured
not so much by the position
that one has reached in life
as by the obstacles
which he has overcome
while trying to succeed.

Booker T. Washington

INSURANCE POLICY

Any time the future looks too gray,
I have an atticful of yesterday.

Florence B. Jacobs

Keep your face to the sunshine
and you cannot see the shadow.

Helen Keller

Joy freed from the bond
of earth's slumber
rushes into numberless leaves,
and dances in the air
for a day.

Rabindranath Tagore

Instead of lamenting
the absurdity of the world,
let us try to transform
the corner of it
into which we were born.

André Maurois

LIFE IS FOR LIVING

How lovely the days
　　When sunlight comes streaming,
　　How exquisite the nights
　　When starshine is gleaming.
　　How delightful are meadows
　　With wild flowers blooming,
　　Or roses entwining,
　　The breezes perfuming;

　　How welcome a gentle rain
　　Falling in springtime.
　　How happy the children
　　At seesaw and swing-time
　　When they can run free
　　Waving crimson balloons,
　　Chasing butterflies, newly-emerged
　　From cocoons;

　　How graceful are swans
　　As they're gliding and swimming,
　　How enchanting are sea gulls
　　All dipping and skimming.
　　How vast heaven's dome
　　For flying a kite in;
　　How wondrous the world is
　　To love and delight in!

Katherine Nelson Davis

W hat a new face courage puts on everything!

Ralph Waldo Emerson

A RECIPE FOR HAPPINESS

Take the *wonderful* of flowers
And the *fun* of "Come along!"
Add the *nice surprise* of rainbows
And the *cheerful* of a song...
Take the *kindness* of "How are you?"
And the *friendly* of "Hello!"
And mix with *smiles* and *handshakes*
        from everyone you know,
Toss in *laughter* from together,
The *remember* in apart,
And you'll have the sunshine feeling
        of *happy* in your heart!

Barbara Kunz Loots

I f there were dreams to sell
        What would you buy?

Thomas Lovell Beddoes

56

To me, every hour of the day and night
is an unspeakably perfect miracle.
Walt Whitman

PERMANENCE

For never star shall set, if it but be
A star of substance and reality,
But it shall shine somehow, somewhere, somewhen,
In undiminished brilliancy again.
No stream is lost in marsh or sand or spray
But it shall flow again in rain or rill someday,
And never bright deed perished from the earth
That shall not rise again in greater worth.
Clara Aiken Speer

EVENING

No one saw the day die;
The lovely sky
    spread out across the West,
Folded the world in beauty and
Then let it go to rest.
Sister Mary Faith, O.S.B.

To love abundantly is to live abundantly,
and to love forever is to live forever.

Henry Drummond

LOVELY WORLD

Lazy day,
Sun bright,
Every single thing
Just right,
Happy heart,
A budding tree,
Hum of springtime
Bumblebee,
A yellow carpet
On the ground —
Dandelions
All around…
Perfect world
That children play in,
And I can spend
The golden day in!

Katherine Nelson Davis

Have courage for the great sorrows of life
and patience for the small ones.
And when you have finished your daily task,
go to sleep in peace. God is awake.

Victor Hugo

GIVING

The happiness I give
Does not deplete my store;
I freely give and find
That I have more and more!

A small kind deed I chanced
To do as I passed by
Brought hope anew. Thus small
Deeds live and multiply.

I'm not afraid to spend
Myself; thus comes my strength.
That spent and given is
The all I'll own at length!

Gracie Cornett

E ven if I knew that tomorrow
the world would go to pieces,
I would still plant my apple tree.

Martin Luther